Encounters with God

The Epistle of Paul
the Apostle to the
EPHESIANS

Encounters with God

The Epistle of Paul the Apostle to the EPHESIANS

Published in Nashville, Tennessee, by Thomas Nelson. Thomas Nelson is a registered
trademark of Thomas Nelson, Inc.

Thomas Nelson, Inc. titles may be purchased in bulk for educational, business,
fund-raising, or sales promotional use. For information, please e-mail
SpecialMarkets@ThomasNelson.com.

All Scripture quotations are taken from THE NEW KING JAMES VERSION.
© 1982 by Thomas Nelson, Inc. Used by permission. All rights reserved.

ISBN 978-1-4185-2647-4

Printed in the United States of America

08 09 10 11 12 RRD 5 4 3 2 1

CONTENTS

CONTENTS

AN INTRODUCTION TO THE EPISTLE OF EPHESIANS

The Book of Ephesians is an "epistle"—a formal letter intended to give instruction. The letter was written by the apostle Paul to the early-church believers in Ephesus, a major city in the Roman province of Asia (present-day Turkey).

Paul knew the Ephesians well. He had lived among them for three years, teaching those who had come to Christ under his evangelistic ministry, and also perhaps, those who had come to Christ under the ministry of the apostle John. Paul first went to the city on his second missionary journey, and left Priscilla and Aquila (his tent making associates) behind to continue the work he started. On his third missionary journey, during which Paul remained in Ephesus for three years (Acts 19:1–41), his ministry was marked by numerous miracles and conversions, to the point that local artisans who made idols for pagan worship felt threatened by Paul's ministry and sought to persecute him greatly.

Paul wrote to the Ephesians from a prison cell many years after his stay in Ephesus. At the time he wrote, he had been taken into official custody in Rome, setting the date of the letter close to 60 AD.

Ephesus was one of the most prominent and elegant cities of the first century. It had a major sheltered port and was located on several significant trade routes—including the famous "silk route" and "spice route." This harbor has long since been filled with silt and the ruins of ancient Ephesus are now several miles from the Mediterranean Sea. In the first century, however, the city was a major commercial center, with a very large slave market and an international population. The city was famous for its temple to the fertility goddess Diana, which was considered one of the seven wonders of the ancient world. Excavations of the city have revealed a significant four-story, marble-façade library, streets made of marble, shopping streets with intricate mosaic sidewalks, elaborate public baths and entertainment arenas, an amphitheatre that seated ten thousand people (with perfect acoustics), and homes with exotic court yards and an early form of air conditioning produced by a series of fans funneling air through conduits. The city was wealthy, cosmopolitan, and for the most part, pagan.

Ephesus was also the city which the apostle John used as a headquarters. Many believe it is the place to which Mary, the mother of Jesus, traveled with John and lived out the remainder of her life.

The letter Paul wrote to the Ephesians was intended to be a circular letter sent to several congregations in Asia, of which Ephesus was the hub city. Some of the ancient versions of the letter do not include the phrase "who are in Ephesus" in the opening verse, and the letter has no personal references, both of which suggest a broader audience.

This letter does not address specific issues, as do many of the other letters of Paul. Rather, the teaching is general in nature and covers several broad theological issues: the grace of God, the calling of the Christian, the unity of believers, and God's eternal purposes revealed through Christ. The letter reflects the maturity of Paul's faith after many years of ministry. Paul presents the full scope of God's eternal plan of salvation and seeks to help believers identify ways in which they fit into God's purposes through their faith in Christ Jesus. He refers to the church as a building (2:19–22), Christ's body (1:22, 23), Christ's bride (5:23), a new people (2:14, 15), and as soldiers prepared for spiritual battle (6:10–20).

The book is a blend of both doctrine, and practical ethical Christian living. Paul advocates repeatedly the need to "put off the old life" and "put on Christ." Paul makes it very clear that we who are Christians have a purpose in our world today, we belong fully to one another and to God as adopted children in His eternal family, and we have been given everything we need to live a victorious Christian life.

Perhaps more than any other epistle, Ephesians presents the portrait of a strong, healthy, and effective church.

About the Author, the Apostle Paul. Paul's name was originally Saul (Acts 13:9), the royal name of Israel's first king. Upon his conversion, he adopted the name Paul, which literally meant "little" and reflected his self-evaluation as being "the least of the apostles" (1 Corinthians 15:98). Certainly in the history of Christianity, the "little" apostle became the foremost apostle to the Gentile world.

Paul was a Roman citizen, his hometown being Tarsus, the chief city of Cilicia. He was fluent in Greek, studied philosophy and theology under Gamaliel, and was also a Hebrew, the son of a Pharisee from the tribe of Benjamin. Paul, too, became a Pharisee, a very strict follower of Jewish religious laws. By trade, he was a tentmaker. This unique blend of cultural, religious, and experiential factors gave Paul unusual entrée into both Gentile and Jewish circles. This was especially important in an international trade center such as Ephesus.

Initially, Paul was a major force in denouncing Christianity in Jerusalem, and had been a willing witness to Stephen's martyrdom. While on a mission to seek out and destroy Christians who had traveled to Syria, Paul had a dramatic encounter with the risen Christ and in the aftermath, became as zealous a believer in Christ Jesus and advocate for the Gospel as he once had been a zealous foe to the early church. He took several fruitful and demanding missionary journeys, spending as long as two years in some areas to teach those who had heeded the Gospel message and accepted Jesus as their Savior. Over the decades of his ministry, he became the most influential church planter and theologian in the early church. His letters addressed both the triumphs and difficulties encountered by the first-century Christians, many of whom faced intense persecution for their faith.

The issues Paul addressed in his letters to the first-century church are no less important to today's believers. Paul laid a very practical foundation for *how* to live the Christian life, even in the face of struggles, temptations, and heresies. His personal example of seeking to know and obey Christ Jesus no matter the cost, remains an example to all who call themselves Christians. "I in Christ and Christ in me" was Paul's unwavering theme song.

AN OVERVIEW OF OUR STUDY
OF THE EPISTLE OF EPHESIANS

This study guide presents seven lessons drawn from and based largely upon the Epistle of Ephesians. The study guide elaborates upon, and is based upon, the commentary included in the *Blackaby Study Bible:*

Lesson #1: Gifted with Spiritual Wisdom

Lesson #2: Saved by Faith, Not Works

Lesson #3: United in Christ

Lesson #4: Equipped for Ministry

Lesson #5: Walking in Newness of Life

Lesson #6: Submitted to One Another

Lesson #7: Fully Armed for Spiritual Battle

Personal or Group Use. These lessons are offered for personal study and reflection, or for small-group Bible study. The questions asked may be answered by an individual reader, or used as a foundation for group discussion. A segment titled "Notes to Leaders of Small Groups" is included at the back of this book to help those who might lead a group study of the material here.

Before you embark on this study, we encourage you to read in full the statement in the Blackaby Study Bible titled "How to Study the Bible." Our contention is always that the Bible is unique among all literature. It is God's definitive word for humanity. The Bible is:

- *inspired*—"God breathed"

- *authoritative*—absolutely the "final word" on any spiritual matter

- *the plumb line of truth*—the standard against which all human activity and reasoning must be evaluated

The Bible is fascinating in that it has remarkable diversity, but also remarkable unity. The books were penned by a diverse assortment of authors representing a variety of languages and cultures. The Bible as a whole has a number of literary forms. But, the Bible's message from cover to cover is clear, consistent, and unified.

More than mere words on a page, the Bible is an encounter with God Himself. No book is more critical to your life. The very essence of the Bible is the Lord Himself speaking to you today through His Word.

God speaks by the Holy Spirit through the Bible. He also communicates during your time of prayer, in your life circumstances, and through the church. Read your Bible in an attitude of prayer, and allow the Holy Spirit to make you aware of God's activity in and your personal life. Write down what you learn, meditate on it, and adjust your thoughts, attitudes, and behavior accordingly. Look for ways every day in which the truth of God's Word can be applied to your circumstances and relationships. God is not random, but orderly and intentional in the way He speaks to you.

Be encouraged—the Bible is *not* too difficult for the average person to understand if that person asks the Holy Spirit for help. (Furthermore, not even the most brilliant person can fully understand the Bible apart from the Holy Spirit's help!) God desires for you to know Him and to know His Word. Every person who reads the Bible can learn from it. The person who will receive *maximum* benefit from reading and studying the Bible, however, is the person who is:

- *born again* (John 3:3, 5). Those who are born again and have received the gift of His Spirit have a greater capacity to understand the deeper truths of God's Word.

- *a heart that desires to learn God's truth.* Your attitude influences greatly the outcome of Bible study. Resist the temptation to focus on what others have said about the Bible. Allow the Holy Spirit to guide you as you study God's Word for yourself.

- *a heart that seeks to obey God.* The Holy Spirit teaches most those who have a desire to apply what they learn.

Begin your Bible study with prayer, asking the Holy Spirit to guide your thoughts and to impress upon you what is on God's heart. Then, make plans to adjust your life immediately to obey the Lord fully.

As you read and study the Bible, your purpose is not to *create* meaning, but to *discover* the meaning of the text as the Holy Spirit reveals God's truth. Ask yourself, "What did the author have in mind? How was this applied by those who first heard these words?" Especially in your study of the Gospel accounts, pay attention to the words of Jesus that begin "truly, truly" or "He opened His mouth and taught them saying." These are core principles and teachings that have powerful impact on *every* person's life.

At times you may find it helpful to consult other passages of the Bible (made available in the center columns in the Blackaby Study Bible), or the commentary that is in the margins of the Blackaby Study Bible.

Keep in mind always that Bible study is not primarily an exercise for acquiring information, but an opportunity for transformation. Bible study is your opportunity to encounter God and to be changed in His presence. When God speaks to your heart, nothing remains the same. Jesus said, "He who has ears to hear, let him hear" (Matt. 13:9). Choose to have ears that desire to hear!

The B-A-S-I-Cs of Each Study in This Guide. Each lesson in this study guide has five segments, using the word BASIC as an acronym. The word BASIC does not allude to elementary or "simple," but rather, to "foundational." These studies extend the concepts that are part of the Blackaby Study Bible commentary and are focused on key aspects of what it means to be a Christ-follower in today's world. The BASIC acronym stands for:

B = Bible Focus. This segment presents the central passage for the lesson and a general explanation that covers the central theme or concern.

A = Application for Today. This segment has a story or illustration related to modern-day times, with questions that link the Bible text to today's issues, problems, and concerns.

S = Supplementary Scriptures to Consider. In this segment, other Bible verses related to the general theme of the lesson are explored.

I = Introspection and Implications. In this segment, questions are asked that lead to deeper reflection about one's personal faith journey and life experiences.

C = Communicating the Good News. In this segment, challenging questions are aimed at ways in which the truth of the lesson might be lived out and shared with others (either to win the lost or build up the church).

LESSON #1
GIFTED WITH SPIRITUAL WISDOM

Wisdom: knowledge and experience to make Godly decisions and judgments; to determine the mind of Christ

B
Bible Focus

> *Therefore I also, after I heard of your faith in the Lord Jesus and your love for all the saints, do not cease to give thanks for you, making mention of you in my prayers: that the God of our Lord Jesus Christ, the Father of glory, may give to you the spirit of wisdom and revelation in the knowledge of Him, the eyes of your understanding being enlightened; that you may know what is the hope of His calling, what are the riches of the glory of His inheritance in the saints, and what is the exceeding greatness of His power toward us who believe, according to the working of His mighty power which He worked in Christ when He raised Him from the dead and seated Him at His right hand in the heavenly places, far above all principality and power and might and dominion, and every name that is named, not only in this age but also in that which is to come.*
>
> *And He put all things under His feet, and gave Him to be head over all things to the church, which is His body, the fullness of Him who fills all in all (Ephesians 1:15–23).*

We live in an information age, a time in which no one person can possibly begin to know all of the facts that are available to know. Beyond knowledge, which is rooted in fact, lies understanding—which tells a person when, how, where, with whom, and for what purposes to use knowledge. And beyond understanding lies wisdom—which tells a person *why* certain things are true or false, and the relevance of specific information. Natural wisdom pertains to knowledge and understanding of our physical, fleshly, and material world. Spiritual wisdom pertains to the things of God, including God's overall plans and purposes for humanity.

Paul is very specific in writing to the Ephesians about the scope of spiritual wisdom and revelation, which he terms "enlightened understanding." His desire is that the Ephesians will know these three things specifically:

• *The hope of His calling.* This hope, for Paul, was the hope of resurrected, everlasting life. This hope was not a whim or a wish, but a hope rooted in deep assurance that because the eternal Spirit of God resides in the believer, the believer will not only live forever but be fully transformed into the likeness of Christ Jesus. Paul wanted the Ephesians, and *us*, to be fully convinced that everything in our lives is aimed toward that ultimate fullness of life and richness of purpose. When a person truly sees this present life in the context of eternity, life takes on different meaning. We catch a glimpse of God's "big plan" for us and for all humanity. We have insight into both the reason for our existence on this earth and our present challenges. The hope of eternal life becomes the context for spiritual wisdom.

- *The riches of the glory of His inheritance in the saints.* Note that Paul did not say the riches of the glory for the saints. Rather, Paul wrote that the saints are the riches of the glory of *Christ's* inheritance. What a wonderful statement this is about the *value* of every Christian believer! The Lord sees us as the crowning achievement of His death, resurrection, and gift of the Holy Spirit. Our value to Him is beyond measure—God longs to live with us forever and to pour out His love and blessings upon our earthly lives. He *treasures* us. When we see ourselves as truly valuable to the Lord, we govern our lives in a new way. Just as a child who knows he is adored by his earthly father seeks to become as much like that earthly father as possible, and to please his father in all things, so we who know we are adored and are valuable to our Heavenly Father seek to please our Heavenly Father in all things and become as much like Jesus as possible. Knowing that we are the "riches of the glory of His inheritance" gives us a motivating desire for spiritual wisdom.

- *The exceeding greatness of His power toward us who believe.* Throughout his writings, Paul assured the believers in Christ that the Spirit had been given to them to empower them—to preach and teach the Gospel with authority and compelling conviction, to work miracles, and to overturn the works of evil whenever they were encountered. Paul taught that God's unlimited power is poured through our limited lives with a fullness that can only be identified as "exceeding" our capacity. This means that God is always available to us, always working in us, and always working through us and on our behalf. Fully understanding that God is *using* us, and at the same time, is transforming us, gives us boldness in acting on what we know to be true.

Above all else, spiritual wisdom is rooted in knowing who Jesus really *is*. He is the One who was raised from the dead, ascended into heaven, and is seated at the right hand of the Father. In this position of supreme honor, He has all authority over all God's creation and is worthy of all praise. He is the head of the Church, His body. He governs all activity of the Church, even as He fulfills the plan and purpose for every person in the Church.

Our challenge is to *know* Christ. Not just with head knowledge, but experiencing Him in our daily lives. For in knowing Him, we have everything we ultimately need to know. In understanding who we are to Him, and who He desires to be to us, we have an understanding of that which is eternal in perspective. Once we understand our position in Christ, we know how to order our lives and give meaning to our days. We truly are capable of seeing our world and our own lives through "eyes of enlightened understanding."

Are you praying for spiritual wisdom and revelation for yourself?

Are you praying, as Paul prayed, for others around you to have spiritual wisdom and revelation of Christ Jesus?

A
Application for Today

Most school-aged children at some point receive a poor grade on a test or project. One bad grade usually doesn't mean much. But a string of poor grades, and especially a pattern of poor grades in a variety of subjects, can lead a child to conclude, "I'm dumb. I'm not cut out for school." Discouragement furthers the downward spiral—such a student tends to study less, ceases to care, and may even drop out of school (emotionally and intellectually even if he continues to attend classes).

Adults are not immune from this process. A string of failures in the workplace —perhaps the repeated loss of jobs—can lead a person to conclude, "I'm a failure. I'll never be successful." Again, such conclusions can lead to a downward spiral marked by less effort, less concern with productivity, quality, or efficiency in working, and perhaps even permanent unemployment or employment in jobs that seem less and less satisfying.

But what about the church? What happens when a person reads the Bible and just doesn't seem to understand it? Does that person tend to read more or less?

What happens when everybody else in the church seems to know Bible verses and Bible stories, and the new convert does not? Does he feel included or excluded from the Body?

What happens when a person isn't welcomed into a church body? Does that person attend church more or less frequently?

What happens when a person doesn't seem to understand what others in the church "know"—either about how to navigate through a church service, the terms used in describing spiritual behavior, or why certain things are done as they are done? Does that person press to learn more, or withdraw?

What happens when a new convert becomes discouraged that he just can't seem to "be good enough for the church"?

S
Supplementary Scriptures to Consider

Paul also wrote this to the Ephesians:

> Therefore do not be unwise, but understand what the will of
> the Lord is (Ephesians 4:17).

• We often tend to think in terms of the "will of the Lord" as something
we DO. Reflect for a moment on what the Lord wills you to BE.

• How might you better pursue the will of the Lord for your life?

True spiritual wisdom and understanding comes as we seek to know and
to obey God's commands to us—both as the Bible gives us God's commandments, and as the Holy Spirit enlightens our minds to understand His
commandments and how to live them out in our world today:

> For the LORD gives wisdom;
> From His mouth come knowledge and understanding;
> He stores up sound wisdom for the upright;
> He is a shield to those who walk uprightly;
> He guards the paths of justice,
> And preserves the way of His saints.
> Then you will understand righteousness and justice,
> Equity and every good path (Proverbs 2:6–9).

• Many people believe that the only commands of God that they need to know are the Ten Commandments. How does the Lord command you in an ongoing way, from day to day? What do you hear coming from the Lord's "mouth" that gives you knowledge and understanding about how to live your life in an "upright" way?

• How is it that we understand righteousness, justice, equity, and every good path, only as we *obey* what God directs us to do and be?

The psalmist wrote:

> "Give me understanding,
> That I may know Your testimonies (Psalm 119:125).

• We sometimes speak of having "God moments" or refer to things that happen as "God events." What testifies to you that God is involved in a particular situation?

• Is there anything that happens in our lives or in creation that does *not* give testimony to God's goodness, greatness, and involvement? Why do we seem blind to the full spectrum of God's "testimonies" all around us?

• In what way do we grow spiritually—understanding more about the nature of God and more about the ways He works in us and in others— as we share our faith stories with others, and hear their faith stories in return?

The writer of Proverbs had this to say about our gaining genuine spiritual wisdom and understanding:

> He who heeds the word wisely will find good
>   (Proverbs 16:20).
> The wise in heart will be called prudent (Proverbs 16:21).
> Understanding is a wellspring of life to him who has it
>   (Proverbs 16:22).
> The heart of the wise teaches his mouth (Proverbs 16:23).

- Reflect on each of these statements from Proverbs. Note what these phrases or words mean to you with regard to acquiring spiritual wisdom:
  HEEDS THE WORD—
  PRUDENCE—
  WELLSPRING OF LIFE—
  HEART...TEACHES HIS MOUTH—

I
Introspection and Implications

1. Without consulting a dictionary or Bible commentary, how would you explain to another person:
   THE HOPE YOU HAVE IN CHRIST JESUS—
   THE WORTH YOU FEEL IN CHRIST JESUS—
   THE POWER YOU EXPERIENCE AS A RESULT OF BELIEVING IN CHRIST JESUS—

2. How much do you feel a *need* for greater spiritual wisdom?

3. What are you doing to acquire greater spiritual wisdom?

4. What do you believe will be the evidence of greater spiritual wisdom in your life?

C
Communicating the Good News

The apostle Paul also called us to wisdom in the way we relate to and communicate with lost souls:

> Walk in wisdom toward those who are outside, redeeming the time. Let your speech always be with grace, seasoned with salt, that you may know how you ought to answer each one (Colossians 4:5–6).

What does it mean to you to "redeem the time" when it comes to sharing Christ with others?

What does it mean to you to have your speech reflect *grace*?

What does it mean for your words to be *seasoned with salt*?

To what degree do you feel equipped to answer the questions, or respond to the remarks, of unsaved friends and acquaintances? How might you become better equipped?

LESSON #2
SAVED BY FAITH, NOT WORKS

Saved: to be forgiven and receive the gift of eternal life; conversely, to be spared punishment for sins and eternal death

B
Bible Focus

> *And you He made alive, who were dead in trespasses and sins, in which you once walked according to the course of this world, according to the prince of the power of the air, the spirit who now works in the sons of disobedience, among whom also we all once conducted ourselves in the lusts of our flesh, fulfilling the desires of the flesh and of the mind, and were by nature children of wrath, just as the others.*
>
> *But God, who is rich in mercy, because of His great love with which He loved us, even when we were dead in trespasses, made us alive together with Christ (by grace you have been saved), and raised us up together, and made us sit together in the heavenly places in Christ Jesus, that in the ages to come He might show the exceeding riches of His grace in His kindness toward us in Christ Jesus. For by grace you have been saved through faith, and that not of yourselves; it is the gift of God, not of works, lest anyone should boast. For we are His workmanship, created in Christ Jesus for good works, which God prepared beforehand that we should walk in them (Ephesians 2:1–10).*

We are saved—our sins forgiven and our eternal home in heaven assured—by what *Jesus* accomplished, not by what *we* accomplish.

The word "grace" in the Greek language (*charis*) denotes kindness, benefit, or goodwill. It evokes images of a superior granting favor to an undeserving inferior. The Lord's grace includes the wonderful concepts of undeserved favor, unexpected acceptance, and unconditional love.

It is fully in accordance with God's grace that God created a means for us to come back into right relationship with Him and be fully forgiven of our sins. It is an act of God's grace that when we confess with our mouths that Jesus is the Savior, we are granted the gift of eternal life (See Romans 10:8–10 and John 3:16).

The means of our salvation seems "too easy" to some people. We in Western Civilization tend to be achievement-oriented. We pride ourselves on what we can do and accomplish—most of our standards related to "success" point toward position within a company or society that we have earned, the depth of our financial portfolio, the homes and other material items we have purchased, and at times, even the spouse and children we have. We see these things and people as something we have acquired, at least to some degree, according to our ability, likeability, or maneuverability.

Simply to "believe and receive" seems to some as if God is doing everything and we are doing nothing.

Precisely.

In truth, what could you possibly *do* to be good enough for God? How good would you have to be? How much would you have to do? How would you know?

God does not ask us to strive. He does not insist that we "arrive." He loves us as we are and offers to help us become all that we have already been created to be. He offers to receive us as we are, if we are willing to receive His Son.

It is not our nature—no matter how good we may think we are—that saves us. It is God's infinitely loving, freely forgiving nature that reaches out to us.

It is not how high we can reach toward heaven. It is how low Heaven has already reached toward us.

But what about those who claim that we have to do *nothing* to receive God's grace? To the contrary! Our part is to believe and receive. And why, you may ask, is this not a "work"? Because work, by its very definition, implies some form of effort or exertion. Work produces accomplishment. Nothing about our believing and receiving involves human effort, exertion, or accomplishment. It is not "work" for a healthy person to inhale, to receive into their lungs the air around them. At the same time, inhaling oxygen involves human willingness to inhale. A man can purse his lips and refuse to breathe. A person who does not seek oxygen in an oxygen-void vacuum will die. In a similar manner, a person who does not willfully believe and receive Christ Jesus after hearing the Gospel faces eternal death. We cannot "win" our salvation through human intelligence or good deeds. But we must "accept" what has been freely offered to us.

A
Application for Today

"I just don't know what you mean," the young man explained to his friend as they walked toward their college classroom.

"About what?" the friend replied.

"Being saved," he said. "What on earth do you mean when you continually talk about being saved or getting saved? Saved from *what?*"

"From your sinful nature," the friend said.

"What makes you think I have a sinful nature?" the young man asked with a laugh.

"Because everybody has a sinful nature," the friend said seriously. "God wants you to turn to Him and accept Jesus as your Savior, so Jesus can change your sinful nature and free you from the guilt of your sins."

"What if I don't feel guilty?" the young man said with a nervous laugh. And then as if to divert the focus from himself, he pointed out to his friend, "You still sin."

The friend paused for a moment. "Yes," he admitted, "I do. But I don't want to, and when I do sin, I turn immediately to God and ask Him to forgive me and I know He does."

"How do you know he forgives?"

"Because I have believed in Jesus Christ—I have believed that Jesus died on the cross as the sacrifice for my sin. Jesus died so I don't have to sin, don't have to feel guilty, and so I won't die eternally because I have sinned."

"Do you really believe that stuff about hell?" the young man asked.

"I do."

"Why?"

"Because Jesus taught a lot about hell. If Jesus believed in hell, I believe in it."

"But how does believing in Jesus change me?" the young man asked.

"I don't know HOW He does it," the friend said. "I just know that He does when we believe He is God's Son and receive what He did on the cross as being for our sakes."

Just at that moment a bell rang calling the young men to their classroom. The friend said later to his father, "I felt as if the Savior saved me by the bell today. Dad, I need to know more about how to explain the words I use. I'm just glad this guy didn't ask me why Jesus had to *die* on the cross! Most people don't get that part about shed blood."

How do you explain your salvation to a person who may never have heard the Gospel of Jesus Christ?

Are you aware of the "religious words" that you may use in talking about your salvation—words that the unsaved person may not understand?

S
Supplementary Scriptures to Consider

The apostle Paul wrote to the Romans that every person has the *ability* to believe and receive Christ Jesus:

God has dealt to each one a measure of faith (Romans 12:3).

• What does the phrase "measure of faith" mean to you?

• Do some people seem to have a greater ability to believe than others?

• Does our capacity to believe grow over time, the more we trust God and the more we seek to receive God's presence in our lives?

Paul wanted the Ephesians to know with certainty that "believing" was all that was necessary to have their sins forgiven:

> If Abraham was justified by works, he has something to boast
> about, but not before God. For what does the Scripture say?
> "Abraham believed God, and it was accounted to him for
> righteousness." Now to him who works, the wages are not
> counted as grace but as debt. But to him who does not work
> but believes on Him who justifies the ungodly, his faith is
> accounted for righteousness, just as David also describes the

blessedness of the man to whom God imputes righteousness
apart from works:

"Blessed are those whose lawless deeds are forgiven,
  And whose sins are covered;
  Blessed is the man to whom the LORD shall not impute sin."
    (Psalm 32:1–2) . . .

For the promise that he would be the heir of the world was not to Abra-
ham or to his seed through the law, but through the righteousness of faith
(Romans 4:2–8, 13).

• What specific *spiritual* blessings have you experienced since you received
  Jesus Christ as your Savior? (For example, freedom from guilt, freedom
  from a desire to sin, greater ability to withstand temptation.)

• Why is it impossible for a person to generate these spiritual blessings
  through their own efforts or works?

We human beings like to admire the work of our hands, and to gaze at the
certificates of achievement on our walls. The New Testament says this to us:

Now faith is the substance of things hoped for, the evidence of
things not seen . . . (Hebrews 11:1).

• How difficult is it to believe in things we cannot see, touch, or otherwise experience by our natural senses?

• Respond to this statement: "In Christianity, it's not seeing that produces believing, but believing that produces seeing." What are some things we simply cannot understand about God, or ourselves, until we first believe that Jesus is Savior and Lord of our lives?

I
Introspection and Implications

1. In fifty words or less, how do you tell an unsaved person about their need for Christ Jesus?

2. Without consulting a dictionary or Bible commentary, how do you define these words or phrases:
   SAVED—
   GRACE—
   WORKS—
   ATONING SACRIFICE OF CHRIST—
   SUBSTITUTIONARY SACRIFICE OF CHRIST—

3. Think back to your own salvation experience. What was involved? How did you know with certainty that you had been saved? What changed in your life?

4. What does it mean to you to read these words of Paul: "For we are His workmanship, created in Christ Jesus for good works."

C
Communicating the Good News

The New Testament tells us about the creative ongoing work of God as we give voice to our faith:

> By faith we understand that the worlds were framed by the
> word of God, so that the things which are seen were not made
> of things which are visible (Hebrews 11:3).

In what ways have you experienced God creating as you have spoken His word to other people? How does speaking the word of God's forgiveness and love produce a new environment, cause people to think in new ways about God, or create a new opportunity for spiritual growth?

Why is the free gift of salvation *always* the heartbeat of genuine evangelism?

Lesson #3

UNITED IN CHRIST

Our Peace: wholeness of spirit, soul, body, and relationships

B
Bible Focus

> Now in Christ Jesus you who once were far off have been
> brought near by the blood of Christ.
> For He Himself is our peace, who has made both one, and
> has broken down the middle wall of separation, having
> abolished in His flesh the enmity, that is, the law of command-
> ments contained in ordinances, so as to create in Himself one
> new man from the two, thus making peace, and that He might
> reconcile them both to God in one body through the cross,
> thereby putting to death the enmity. And He came and
> preached peace to you who were afar off and to those who
> were near. For through Him we both have access by one Spirit
> to the Father.
> Now, therefore, you are no longer strangers and foreigners,
> but fellow citizens with the saints and members of the house-
> hold of God, having been built on the foundation of the
> apostles and prophets, Jesus Christ Himself being the chief
> cornerstone, in whom the whole building, being fitted together,
> grows into a holy temple in the Lord, in whom you also are
> being built together for a dwelling place of God in the Spirit
> (Ephesians 2:13–22).

We human beings often struggle with a sense of isolation and an inner
emotional feeling of disconnectedness. We long for closeness with other
human beings, and also with God.

What keeps us from connecting with others? In part, our differences—
which manifest themselves in different traditions, cultures, tribes, and
nations. These differences can easily turn into suspicion or jealousy of
others, prejudice against others, and even hatred toward others. As differences are exaggerated and may become associated with problems, they
divide us even further. Certainly no two groups of people—culturally or in
their religion—could have been any more different than first-century Jews
and Gentiles. The Gentiles of Ephesus were worldly, sophisticated, and
international, but no less "ungodly" in the eyes of the Jews who lived in the
city. The worship of the Greek goddess Diana permeated the city, accompa-
nied by much prostitution and fortune-telling. Thousands of books filled the
main library of Ephesus, but very likely none of them were a scroll of the
Torah, the sacred writings of Judaism. For their part, the Gentiles likely
looked upon Jewish customs as primitive and inflexible.

But now, these two very diverse groups of people are bound together in the same church! What a miracle...and what a challenge!

What is it that has bound the Ephesian Jews and Gentiles together? Paul spells it out clearly: the reconciliation made possible by Jesus Christ on the cross. Both Jews and Gentiles have been reunited with the same God, and in that, they share the same peace with God and have been granted the same access to God by the same Spirit of God.

Their commonality is in what Jesus has done for them, not in what they have done for Christ or what they have done for or with one another.

It is Christ Jesus who is making you into the same household, and creating out of you one temple, Paul wrote. He said this, of course, to people who lived in the shadow of one of the seven wonders of the ancient world—the large and overpowering temple to Diana set on the highest hill in Ephesus. The metaphor that Paul used was not lost on the Ephesians. He regarded their very existence as the true "wonder of God" in the world—and saw them as a lasting and eternal edifice that transcended anything man might be able to build.

We should also note that the church in Ephesus was not small. A number of scholars have calculated that as many as ten thousand Christians lived in Ephesus by the end of Paul's stay there—this was a large church. The believers met together on special days in the magnificent amphitheater in Ephesus, and at other times, in smaller home groups. The organization of the church was not unlike that of many large churches today. It is easy, as any pastor of a very large church knows, for such a church to splinter into cliques and specialized groups. It is not at all unlikely that the church at Ephesus struggled with a tendency to divide into "Jewish believer groups" and "Gentile believer groups." Perhaps for this very reason, Paul reminds the church at Ephesus that it is being "fitted together" by God, as *one* building, *one* body of believers, *one household* of God.

What divides you today from other people?

What divides you from other believers?

What unites you?

Which is more important—what divides or what unites?

A
Application for Today

"She's Korean," the woman said to her husband. "She doesn't understand much English, and I can hardly understand the English she does speak." A Korean family had joined the church and one of their daughters was in this woman's Sunday school class. "I don't know how to help her," the woman said, and then added without thinking, "I wish there was a good Korean church in our city."

"Why?" the woman's son asked. "Would we go to the Korean church if it was better than our church?"

The woman suddenly realized what she had said. Her young son had made a good point without realizing it! She said in reply, "No. I think what we need to do is to make our church Korean-friendly."

"Great!" her son replied. "I think I'm going to try to learn some Korean words."

After their son had left the room, the woman's husband spoke up. "I remember when the first Hispanics came to my school. They didn't speak much English. But Ferd was a good friend of mine through high school until his family moved away."

"Who?" his wife asked.

"Ferdinand Gonzales. We called him Ferd."

Grandpa, who had been in the room but had been silent until now, spoke up. "And I remember when the first blacks moved to our town. They didn't fit in right away, but there was only one church back then in our town so they attended—every Sunday. James and I became friends—I called him Jimbo. He taught me a lot about fishing."

"It's about learning more than Sunday school lessons, isn't it?" the woman said. "I suspect I'm going to be learning as much this year as my students."

"Maybe it's the *main* Sunday school lesson of the year," her husband added.

What is it that we can learn about *Christ* from others who join our churches from different cultural or racial backgrounds?

S
Supplementary Scriptures to Consider

Paul wrote very specifically about becoming one with others in the church:

> Become complete. Be of good comfort, be of one mind, live in peace; and the God of love and peace will be with you
> (2 Corinthians 13:11).

• What does it mean to "become complete" in a church body?

• What does it mean to be "of good comfort"?

• What does it mean to "live in peace"?

• Paul wrote that it is *as* the church becomes of one mind and lives in peace that God's love fills the church. What does this mean to you in a practical way as you think about your own church?

Paul gave this advice to the church in Thessalonica:

> Comfort each other and edify one another, just as you also are
> doing (1 Thessalonians 5:11).

• To edify means to "build up" and encourage in the faith. How do you
  edify others in your church? To what degree—and in what ways—do you
  need to know another's problems, weaknesses, or background to edify
  and encourage with maximum effectiveness?

Paul warned against those things that divide believers:

> Avoid foolish disputes, genealogies, contentions, and strivings
> about the law; for they are unprofitable and useless. Reject a
> divisive man after the first and second admonition, knowing
> that such a person is warped and sinning, being
> self-condemned (Titus 3:9–11).

• In what ways do each of these tend to divide people:
  GENEALOGIES (a concern with ancestry and social standing)—
  CONTENTIONS (differences of opinion)—
  STRIVINGS ABOUT THE LAW (different interpretations about how to apply
  God's commandments)—

• What do you think "foolish disputes" might entail? Can you cite an example or two of a foolish dispute that has involved you, your family, or your church?

• In what ways are many of the disputes in the church a matter of custom or style, rather than a genuine matter of belief, morality, or values? Cite examples.

I
Introspection and Implications

1. Why would you encourage a person to attend your church when there might be many other churches in town?

2. On a scale of 1–10 with 10 being high, how would you rate your church when it comes to unity?

3. If Christ truly calls us to love one another as we love ourselves, what does this mean to the holding of prejudices against people of other cultures or races?

4. To what degree do you consider yourself to be prejudiced against others? In what ways is it almost impossible to see prejudice in one's self? How difficult is it to overcome prejudice? What is required to get beyond prejudice? Is it necessary to give up *all* prejudice? Why or why not?

C
Communicating the Good News

How difficult is it to maintain focus on Jesus when we tell others about our faith or invite them to come to church with us? Why is it imperative that we do so?

In what ways do we as the collective Church seem to be more successful in reaching people of different cultures overseas than we are in reaching people of different cultures who live in our home community? Why does this seem to be so?

What are the specific practical challenges we face in overcoming cultural differences as we reach out to others?

LESSON #4

EQUIPPED FOR MINISTRY

Edification: to be spiritually encouraged and "built up" for strength and endurance

B
Bible Focus

> He Himself gave some to be apostles, some prophets, some
> evangelists, and some pastors and teachers, for the equipping
> of the saints for the work of ministry, for the edifying of the
> body of Christ, till we all come to the unity of the faith and of
> the knowledge of the Son of God, to a perfect man, to the
> measure of the stature of the fullness of Christ; that we should
> no longer be children, tossed to and fro and carried about
> with every wind of doctrine, by the trickery of men, in the
> cunning craftiness of deceitful plotting, but, speaking the truth
> in love, may grow up in all things into Him who is the head—
> Christ— from whom the whole body, joined and knit together
> by what every joint supplies, according to the effective work-
> ing by which every part does its share, causes growth of the
> body for the edifying of itself in love (Ephesians 4:11–16).

This passage gives us special insight into the way the first-century church
may have been organized. There appear to have been three very distinct
types of ministries in effect. First, there were a few apostles who had authority that ran throughout the whole Church. Second, there were prophets and
evangelists who traveled from place to place, preaching the will of God and
proclaiming the Gospel of Christ Jesus. And third, there were pastors and
teachers embedded in a local church. Each type of leader had a distinct role
and set of qualities.

Apostles were required to have seen Jesus and witnessed the Resurrection.
Paul claimed his right as an apostle on the basis that he had encountered the
risen Christ on the road to Damascus. The apostles were those who estab-
lished church doctrine and maintained unity among the churches during the
first decades after Jesus' death, resurrection, and ascension.

Prophets engaged in "forth-telling" the will of God. Their declaration of
God's Word to the people had both current and future application. In forth-
telling the plan and purpose of God, the prophets to some extent fore-told
the future because they announced the consequences that followed if men
obeyed or disobeyed God's will. The earliest book of church administration,
called *Didache: The Teaching of the Twelve Apostles*, gave prophets authority to lead in prayer and administer sacraments (such as baptism, Holy
Communion, and wedding ceremonies), but admonished that they stay only
two to thee days in a congregation and that they refuse to demand money or
a meal.

Evangelists were those who spoke the good news that Jesus is the Savior. They often traveled from place to place as the Spirit would lead them.

Pastors and teachers may have been one "set" of people. They were responsible for teaching the word of God—including the story and teachings of Jesus. As the New Testament books became written and copied, and as letters from apostles were circulated, pastor/teachers were responsible for teaching the truths of these works and the doctrine of the faith to their congregations. Pastor literally means "shepherd" in Latin. Pastor/teachers were responsible for ministering to the spiritual needs of their flock and guarding their congregations from heresy and false prophets.

No one person filled all of these leadership roles. The main job description for all these roles was the same:

- *Equip the saints for the work of ministry.* Ministry is any effort aimed at meeting needs in another person's life. The clergy doesn't do the "work" of ministry alone. Ministry involves everybody in the church.

- *Edify the Body of Christ.* Edification is building up the church in faith and encouraging the believers to honor Christ and follow Him at all times and through all circumstances.

The goal set before all church leaders? A mature body of believers that mirrored the character, likeness, and ministry of Christ Jesus! Very specifically, the believers were to become skilled at evaluating false doctrines and recognizing the deceit of false teachers. They were to be skilled in their handling of the Word and in their evaluation of human behavior.

The way in which all ministry was to be conducted? Speaking the truth in a loving manner.

In just a few sentences, Paul gave a "short course" on church leadership. But what is true not only for church leaders but for all in the church is this overriding word from Paul: we are to trust Christ Jesus to help us work effectively together "by what every joint supplies"—that is, each person giving what he has in the way of talents and insight and resources—and to grow. No church can succeed if just a *few* are doing the bulk of the ministry work, or giving the bulk of what is contributed. No church can grow numerically unless every person in the church is growing spiritually.

What is *your* role in *your* church?

Are you growing personally? As a church?

Are you contributing what the Holy Spirit has given to your life? Are you involved in receiving what the Holy Spirit has done through others?

A
Application for Today

Countless pastors in the church today struggle with burn-out. Why? Because so many of them are expected to "do it all." They are expected to preach stellar sermons Sunday after Sunday, perhaps both Sunday morning and Sunday evening, and perhaps several times on a Sunday morning; teach a good midweek Bible study; make sure the church is kept in good repair, visit the sick, make sure the communication channels run smoothly, counsel those who are preparing for marriage as well as those who are struggling in their marriages or with other issues in life, conduct funerals and comfort the grieving, prepare people for baptism, provide the "agenda" for church services and work with the choir and other musicians for an orderly worship experience, encourage the young people to serve God, make sure all the bills are paid, and work with a lay board that may have very high expectations but little willingness to get involved "hands on."

The vast majority of pastors in our nation have churches with fewer than one hundred members, and virtually no "staff" other than, perhaps, a part-time or full-time secretary who may be a volunteer.

The truth is, no pastor *can* do it all. We err in expecting this.

But what *should* we expect?

What is the role of the pastor/teacher in our congregations today?

What is the role of the prophet or evangelist in the Christian community?

What is the role of those not considered pastoral staff?

And how do we establish these roles in churches, guarding against the "old way" of expecting the pastor to do it all?

S
Supplementary Scriptures to Consider

Paul gave very practical advice about behavior among believers. In many ways, these are practicalities pertaining to ministry in the church:

> And we urge you, brethren, to recognize those who labor
> among you, and are over you in the Lord and admonish you,
> and to esteem them very highly in love for their work's sake.
> Be at peace among yourselves.
> We exhort you, brethren, warn those who are unruly, comfort
> the fainthearted, uphold the weak, be patient with all. See
> that no one renders evil for evil to anyone, but always pursue
> what is good both for yourselves and for all
> (1 Thessalonians 5:12–15).

• How difficult is it to warn an "unruly" person? Why do you believe Paul exhorted the brethren to do so?

• What are practical ways to "uphold the weak"?

• In what ways is it difficult to "be patient with all"? Is there a particular person, or type of personality, with whom you find it difficult to be patient?

• Why is it that we rarely can discern, by ourselves, what is good for both ourselves and for "all"? How might we pursue what might better "build up the body"?

Paul taught that those who are teachers should be compensated by those who are taught:

> Let him who is taught the word share in all good things with him who teaches (Galatians 6:6).

• What is the right way to determine compensation of a clergyman? How does a church determine who should be paid and who should be a volunteer? How are volunteers to be compensated?

Paul taught that those who did not yield to the words of the apostles should be shunned, at least to some degree and for some length of time:

> If anyone does not obey our word in this epistle, note that person and do not keep company with him, that he may be ashamed. Yet do not count him as an enemy, but admonish him as a brother (2 Thessalonians 3:14–15).

• What are the dangers inherent in "shunning" a person? How does this express God's love?

• How might a person be "admonished" as a brother but not counted as an enemy?

Paul wrote this about need-meeting in the church:

> Let our people also learn to maintain good works, to meet urgent needs, that they may not be unfruitful (Titus 3:14).

• What are the "good works" in your church that you believe should be maintained?

- What are the "urgent needs" in your church that need to be met?

- How do the maintaining of good works and the meeting of urgent needs result in "fruitfulness"?

I
Introspection and Implications

1. Have you ever experienced the "call of God" to be in ministry? Was this a call to become part of or to establish a lay ministry? Was it a call to become part of the professional clergy?

2. How much and what kinds of training did you receive to do the "ministry" that you do? Was the training sufficient? Did you learn by someone telling you how to be a minister, or by working alongside and observing a mature believer as he or she engaged in ministry?

3. Do you feel fully equipped to recognize false doctrines? Do you feel fully equipped to discern false teachers or false prophets? In what ways do you feel you might become better equipped?

4. Do you feel edified in your church? Is your faith being built up? Are you being encouraged to take risks with your faith for the benefit of others? In what ways might you become more edified by seeking to edify others?

C
Communicating the Good News

Why is it important to have a healthy church to which we invite the unsaved?

What might you share with fellow believers to edify them?

In what ways might you better "equip" others for the work of ministry? What is the wisdom of training your replacement in lay ministry—sooner rather than later?

LESSON #5
WALKING IN NEWNESS OF LIFE

*Renewal: to infuse with new energy, strength, or enthusiasm; to revitalize
or create a newness of being*

B
Bible Focus

> *This I say, therefore, and testify in the Lord, that you should no longer walk as the rest of the Gentiles walk, in the futility of their mind, having their understanding darkened, being alienated from the life of God, because of the ignorance that is in them, because of the blindness of their heart; who, being past feeling, have given themselves over to lewdness, to work all uncleanness with greediness.'*
>
> *But you have no so learned Christ, if indeed you have heard Him and have been taught by Him, as the truth is in Jesus: that you put off, concerning your former conduct, the old man which grows corrupt according to the deceitful lusts, and be renewed in the spirit of your mind, and that you put on the new man which was created according to God, in true righteousness and holiness.*
>
> *. . . Therefore be imitators of God as dear children. And walk in love, as Christ also has loved us and given Himself for us, an offering and a sacrifice to God for a sweet-smelling aroma.*
>
> *Walk as children of light (for the fruit of the Spirit is in all goodness, righteousness, and truth), finding out what is acceptable to the Lord. And have no fellowship with the unfruitful works of darkness, but rather expose them.*
>
> *. . . See then that you walk circumspectly, not as fools but as wise, redeeming the time, because the days are evil.*
>
> *Therefore do not be unwise, but understand what the will of the Lord is (Ephesians 4:17–24, 5:1–2, 8–11, 15–17).*

Our tendency as human beings is to respond to life on the basis of our natural instincts. In other words, we tend to make choices and respond to situations according to what "feels good" or "what feels right" in the moment. For most of us, this is a response we learned at a very early age and may or may not be right.

The apostle Paul warned strongly against responding to life in this way, however. The Gentiles had been taught "right" and "wrong" in a way that did *not* match God's commandments. He also warned that living by instincts can easily lead to "futility of mind" and "blindness of heart."

What is futility of mind? Things that are futile have no usefulness, effectiveness, purpose, or importance. They have no lasting power or eternal value. To have futility of mind is to have no accurate world view, no vision for what might be accomplished for Christ Jesus, no ideal about how to live as Christ in our world today, and no "long view" that sees all temporal things in the light of eternal consequences. Those with futility of mind are "shallow"—they see only what matters for today, only what relates to their physical comfort, and only what they regard as the acceptable fad or style of the moment.

What is blindness of heart? The heart refers to the "will" of a person, as well as to the emotions of a person. To be "blind" is to fail to see others in need, or to fail to take into account the desires, purposes, or role of another person. It is to be totally self-centered and bent completely on self-gratification.

Paul saw those who were unredeemed Gentiles as living shallow, unproductive, self-serving lives. Rather than imitate this old Gentile conduct, Paul said, become imitators of God. Choose to see life as God sees it and to love other people as God loves them!

How do we keep from responding to life on the basis of our emotional needs, instincts, or self-centered passions? Paul noted two keys:

- *Know what is acceptable to the Lord.* Specifically, Paul encouraged the Ephesians to grow in their understanding about what is good, right, and true in God's eyes. Know what puts a person in right standing with God (righteousness) and what qualifies a person to be used in ministry (holiness).

- *Identify and avoid the "unfruitful works of darkness."* Specifically, Paul warned the Ephesians to gain understanding about what produces spiritual blindness, lewdness, and greediness. He told the Ephesians to "expose" these things and avoid them.

Many of us who have walked with God for many years believe we have a fairly accurate and justifiable understanding of what is good and bad behavior. We need to recognize that while this may be true for us who are "older in the faith," it is not necessarily true for those who are young in their faith. In our culture today, much of what is learned has been from the teachers of television, movies, vile music videos, and unchurched peers.

We have a grave responsibility to teach our young people the "unfruitful works of darkness" and to exalt at the same time, those things that are fully acceptable and desired by the Lord.

What do *you* believe to be unfruitful works of darkness in your culture that need to be exposed and explained to the young people in your community? How might you go about that?

What do *you* believe to be the "acceptable" works—those things that put a person into right standing with God and qualify a person for ministry to others in need? How might you go about teaching those works to others?

Why is it imperative that we become imitators of God, refusing to live as those who are unredeemed?

A
Application for Today

A pastor once asked a member of his church how his life had changed since he had accepted Christ Jesus as his Savior. The man had not accepted Christ until he was forty years old and at the time the pastor asked him this question, he was forty-five. The man replied, "Do you mean how my life changed right after I accepted Christ, or how it has changed over the last five years?"

"Both, I guess," the pastor replied.

"Well, before I got saved I seemed to have a nagging feeling for a couple of years that I needed to make a personal decision about Christ. After I accepted Christ I had an overwhelming sense of joy and deep inner peace," the man said. "I felt as clean and shiny as a brand new penny. I thought I was home free—a straight shot to heaven when my time came and no more nagging feelings."

"But that isn't what happened, is it?" the pastor asked.

"No," the man said. "A couple of weeks after I accepted Christ I began to have a nagging feeling inside me that some of the ways in which I related to other people needed to change. The Lord brought to mind my wife, my children, my partners in business, my other associations. I made some adjustments, some of which weren't all that easy. And then, when I had peace about my relationships I began to have a little nagging feeling that some of my personal habits weren't lining up with my new beliefs. I had to make some changes in where I went and what I did with my leisure time. I also had to give up cigarettes and alcohol completely— I am not saying that everyone ought to be like me, but for whatever reasons God had, I needed to give up all nicotine and alcohol."

"Was that all?" the pastor asked.

"Oh, no," the man said. "After I had made those habit changes—which also weren't all that easy to make, Pastor—I found that there were still more things God seemed to want to change in me. I'd feel conviction about some of the words I was using, and some of the jokes that I was telling. Now, Pastor, these were *clean* joke to me before I was saved. By this time, about two years after I accepted Christ, some of those old jokes were feeling very un-Christlike. I knew I wouldn't tell them in Jesus' presence, and I knew for sure He wouldn't be telling me those jokes. A few of the words I had used fairly routinely also needed to be dropped permanently from my vocabulary."

The man took a deep breath and continued, "Then came the scrubbing of some of my attitudes. My behavior was in line with God's commandments, at least most of the time, and my speech was more godly, but I still had some rotten attitudes and thoughts. It was easy changing my behavior and speech compared to changing my attitudes and thoughts. But I'm working on it."

"And what about your peace and joy?" the pastor asked.

"Oh, that's still there. In fact, I feel even more joy and peace than I felt at the beginning," he said. "Let me tell you, if it wasn't for the joy and peace, and knowing that God was with me all the time, these changes would have been *impossible*."

Now it is your turn to respond to the pastor's question: "How has your life changed since you accepted Jesus as your Savior?"

S
Supplementary Scriptures to Consider

Paul wrote this about our newness of life in Christ Jesus:

> For you were once darkness, but now you are light in the Lord (Ephesians 5:8).

• Most of us think of Jesus as being the Light. But Jesus also said in Matthew 5:14, "You are the light of the world." Paul did not tell the Ephesians they were the light *of* the world or light *to* the world, but that they were light *in the Lord*. What does it mean to you to be "light in the Lord"?

Paul wrote to the Ephesians about specific changes in behavior that were associated with newness of life. Below are three passages on this theme:

> Do not be drunk with wine, in which is dissipation; but be filled with the Spirit (Ephesians 5:18).

> Therefore, putting away lying, "Let each one of you speak truth with his neighbor," for we are members of one another. "Be angry, and do not sin": do not let the sun go down on your wrath, nor give place to the devil. Let him who stole steal no longer, but rather let him labor, working with his hands what is good, that he may have something to give him who has need. Let no corrupt word proceed out of your mouth, but what is good for necessary edification, that it may impart grace to the hearers. And do not grieve the Holy Spirit of God, by whom you were sealed for the day of redemption. Let all bitterness, wrath, anger, clamor, and evil speaking be put away from you, with all malice. And be kind to one another, tender-hearted, forgiving one another, even as God in Christ forgave you (Ephesians 4:25–32).

> But fornication and all uncleanness or covetousness, let it not even be named among you, as is fitting for saints; neither filthiness, nor foolish talking, nor coarse jesting, which are not fitting, but rather giving of thanks. For this you know, that no fornicator, unclean person, nor covetous man, who is an idolater, has any inheritance in the kingdom of Christ and God. Let no one deceive you with empty words, for because of these things the wrath of God comes upon the sons of disobedience. Therefore do not be partakers with them (Ephesians 5:3–7).

• As you have read through these three passages from Ephesians, has any particular word or phrase captured your attention in a special way? What do you believe the Lord may be saying to you?

- What are your working definitions for these terms or phrases Paul used in writing to the Ephesians:

DISSIPATION (ASSOCIATED WITH DRUNKENNESS)—

BE ANGRY AND DO NOT SIN—

NOR GIVE PLACE TO THE DEVIL—

CORRUPT WORDS—

GRIEVE THE HOLY SPIRIT—

UNCLEANNESS—

COVETOUSNESS—

- What behaviors might a person expect from someone who is "tender hearted"?

I

Introspection and Implications

1. Who taught you right from wrong? Did they base what they taught you upon God's Word or upon their own experience? Is what they taught you in line with God's commandments, or in line with the culture as a whole?

2. In what ways do you find it challenging to live a deep, purposeful, other-serving life in a society that has countless examples of "shallow living," "leisure pursuits that have no lasting purpose," and "self-serving products and activities"?

3. Paul wrote this to the Ephesians: "for the fruit of the Spirit is in all goodness, righteousness, and truth." What does this phrase mean to you?

C
Communicating the Good News

What is the first, foremost, and most eternally important change that a lost person needs to make as he comes to Christ?

In what ways does the Holy Spirit work within a new convert to bring about behavioral and attitudinal changes? What is our role as more mature believers in helping a new convert recognize a need for change? How might we better communicate our own stories of transformation and renewed minds?

LESSON #6
SUBMITTED TO ONE ANOTHER

Submission: to yield, especially in times of conflict or decision-making

B
Bible Focus

> *Be filled with the Spirit, speaking to one another in psalms and hymns and spiritual songs, singing and making melody in your heart to the Lord, giving thanks always for all things to God the Father in the name of our Lord Jesus Christ, submitting to one another in the fear of God.*
>
> *Wives, submit to your own husbands, as to the Lord. For the husband is head of the wife, as also Christ is head of the church and He is the Savior of the body. Therefore, just as the church is subject to Christ, so let the wives be to their own husbands in everything.*
>
> *Husbands, love your wives, just as Christ also loved the church and gave Himself for her, that He might sanctify and cleanse her with the washing of water by the word, that He might present her to Himself a glorious church, not having spot or wrinkle or any such thing, but that she should be holy and without blemish. So husbands ought to love their own wives as their own bodies; he who loves his wife loves himself. For no one ever hated his own flesh, but nourishes and cherishes it, just as the Lord does the church. For we are members of His body, of His flesh and of His bones. . . . This is a great mystery, but I speak concerning Christ and the church (Ephesians 5:18–30, 32).*

Being "filled" with the Spirit is intended to be daily and ongoing. The phrase, in the Greek language, does not refer to a one-time event but to a continuous experience. God fully expects every believer to remain under the influence of the Holy Spirit at all times.

Being filled with the Spirit, as Paul wrote to the Ephesians, is associated with two things that most Christians find joyous: music and the giving of thanks. Paul admonished the Ephesians to speak to one another in psalms (likely a reference to singing or reciting one or more of the 150 psalms we have in Scripture, or quoting other God-honoring poetic works of the first century). Hymns are compositions directed toward God or about the majesty of omnipotent, omniscient, omnipresent, all-loving God. Spiritual songs are Spirit-inspired songs that express the Christian experience. Making melody in one's heart refers to having a joyful attitude at all times, being just as joyful as if singing songs that inspire toe-tapping exuberance or feelings of gentle bliss.

Paul also admonished the Ephesians to give thanks always "for all things." How can a person thank God for suffering, tragedy, persecution, or heartbreak? By recognizing that God is *always* in control of all things and that God's purpose for all things in the life of the believer is to glorify Christ and generate eternal reward. Circumstances and situations should never dictate what we express to God. Rather, our relationship to God should be what we voice regardless of circumstances and situations. We can trust God to turn all things to our eternal good—and that most certainly is a truth worthy of our thanksgiving!

Then comes an admonition from Paul that many Christians find less than joyous: "submitting to one another in the fear of God." Most people do not like the word "submit," especially as it relates to other people. We may not find it onerous to submit to God—after all, God is all-powerful, all-wise, all-present, and loving. We often do find it difficult to submit to other people, some of whom may be failures, jerks, unrefined, or immature in our eyes!

Submission is not subservience—it is not laying down our lives like a doormat for others to walk upon us. Submission is *yielding* right-of-way when differences of opinion arise with other believers. It is far better to yield to an oncoming car than to demand right of way and crash! It is far better to yield to another's will than to break a valuable relationship.

Paul quickly adds that our submission to one another is to be "in the fear of God." In other words, God expects this of us because ultimately Christ is Lord over all things and all relationships. We submit to others because we have an awesome awareness that God uses other people to impact our lives for our good.

The good news is that the Spirit enables us to yield to others with graciousness and humility. He allows us to learn from even the most unlikely teachers. He allows us to receive from those who appear to have nothing to give. He allows us to find agreement even with those we regard as having a disagreeable personality. What is our part? To *trust* God to use others to instruct us, even as He seeks to use us to instruct others. Being filled with the Spirit requires an ongoing submission to other believers—it is only *as* we submit our wills to them that we can receive what the Holy Spirit desires to impart through them to us.

Paul gave examples related to marriage. Wives, Paul wrote, are to submit to their own husbands—note that Paul does not say that a woman is to submit to every man she encounters. Husbands are to love their wives—note that Paul does not say that a man must love every woman he meets. Submission is a factor in *relationships*. Wives and husbands each are to relate to the other as Christ relates to the church—with an orderliness of authority, respect, emotional support, protection, provision, and love that produces clear direction, unity of purpose, and an abiding feeling of cohesiveness and peace.

What does this mean to us in practical terms?

God loves to hear us sing His praises.

God loves to hear us voice our thanks to Him as an expression of our reliance upon Him.

God loves for us to submit our lives to other believers so He might use them to bless us, help us, protect us, provide for us, and love us.

A
Application for Today

The last time a woman recalls seeing her father was the night he and her mother had an argument about her custody. They each took one of her arms and almost ripped her apart in their anger at each other, as they each shouted, "She's going to be with me." Finally, the mother pulled her loose and the father, in a drunken stupor, staggered from the house. He committed suicide later that night.

Who won?

Nobody.

Who lost the most?

The little girl.

What happens in a church when people grow angry and insist on having their own way? A tug of war ensues.

Who wins?

Nobody.

Who loses?

Everybody.

The person who loses the most may actually not be present during a church "fight." That person is the unsaved person who is never invited to church, never hears the Gospel, and never experiences any form of Christian benevolence because the believers are so busy defending their individual turf that they fail to hear the heart's cry of the lost.

Parting in peace from those with whom you disagree theologically is one thing. The Holy Spirit can and does bless a decision that upholds the expression of truth in the face of heresy.

Seeking to exert dominance and power over those with whom you disagree is an entirely different issue. The Holy Spirit cannot and does not bless the person who brings about discord and dissension solely for the sake of personal power.

S
Supplementary Scriptures to Consider

In writing to the church at Corinth, Paul called for the believers there to submit themselves to the ministry of those in the household of Stephanas:

> I urge you brethren—you know the household of Stephanas,
> that it is the firstfruits of Achaia, and that they have devoted
> themselves to the ministry of the saints—that you also submit
> to such, and to everyone who works and labors with us
> (1 Corinthians 16:16).
> "God resists the proud,
> But gives grace to the humble"
> Therefore submit to God (James 4:6–7 and Proverbs 3:34).

- Every relationship exists in some form of hierarchy that ultimately leads to the sovereignty of God. For example, in a school setting, students yield to teachers, who yield to principals, who yield to superintendents, who yield to school boards, who yield to those who elected them, and ultimately, all must yield eventually and in eternity to the Spirit of truth from whom all instruction flows toward earth. Consider several relationships in your life. Whom are you "under"? Whom are you "over"?

- Ultimately all submission is to God. How important is it to you to remember that it is God who ultimately is in charge of those who are taking charge over you?

• Paul notes that when we, in our pride, resist those in authority over us, God resists us. When we humble ourselves before those in authority over us, God gives His grace. What is the danger of having God resist us? What is the blessing of having God impart to us His grace?

Paul wrote this about the relationship between the young and the old:

> Likewise you younger people, submit yourselves to your elders. Yes, all of you be submissive to one another, and be clothed with humility (1 Peter 5:5).

• Note, as in our earlier mention of husbands and wives, that Paul did not encourage every young person to submit to every old person, but he does call upon those in the church to submit to *their* elders, both in the natural and spiritual realms. What is to be gained by submitting to those who are *your* elders?

• What is to be lost by refusing to submit to your elders?

Not only are we to submit to people, but to the rule of law:

> Therefore submit yourselves to every ordinance of man for the
> Lord's sake, whether to the king as supreme, or to governors,
> as to those who are sent by him for the punishment of evil-
> doers and for the praise of those who do good. For this is the
> will of God, that by doing good you may put to silence the
> ignorance of foolish men—as free, yet not using liberty as a
> cloak for vice, but as bondservants of God. Honor all people.
> Love the brotherhood. Fear God. Honor the king"
> (1 Peter 2:13–17).

• Why is it important to our Christian witness to keep manmade laws?

• What should be our response to manmade laws that are contrary to God's
laws? Why do we need to be willing to bear any consequences of our
disobedience? In what ways can we trust God as we obey manmade laws
to overrule those laws? What should be our role in seeking to turn bad
laws into good ones?

• How are these two admonitions of Paul related: "fear God" and "honor the king"?

I
Introspection and Implications

1. Have you ever refused to submit to someone in authority over you? What was the result?

2. Have you ever willingly submitted to someone in authority over you, even though you disagreed with their choice, decision, or idea? What was the result?

3. What happens in relationships where submission is not mutual, or where those who are in greater authority refuse to love and nurture, or where those in lesser authority refuse to yield and give respect and support?

4. What should happen in cases where a person issues an ungodly or commandment-breaking order to those who are under his or her authority? Are we to obey those in authority over us without question or without voicing opposition?

5. What happens in cases where someone who was under someone's authority suddenly moves to a position of being "over" that person? How can we best adjust to changes in God's hierarchy of authority?

6. Who is it that has taught us that "submission" has a negative aspect? Why do you think we often regard submission as a sign of weakness? How might this negativity toward the word submission impact our relationships with others?

C
Communicating the Good News

When a person comes to Christ Jesus, a submission of personal pride is always involved. The lost person is admitting he is lost. He is admitting he needs a Savior—he cannot save himself. He is yielding to God's rule over his life. Are we wise to acknowledge this submission as something *good*? Should we perhaps acknowledge more often this aspect of submission as it relates to salvation?

Lesson #7

FULLY ARMED FOR SPIRITUAL BATTLE

Wiles: tricks, deceits, cunning ruses and schemes

B
Bible Focus

> *Finally, my brethren, be strong in the Lord and in the power of His might. Put on the whole armor of God, that you may be able to stand against the wiles of the devil. For we do not wrestle against flesh and blood, but against principalities, against powers, against the rulers of the darkness of this age, against spiritual hosts of wickedness in the heavenly places. Therefore take up the whole armor of God, that you may be able to withstand in the evil day, and having done all, to stand.*
>
> *Stand therefore, having girded your waist with truth, having put on the breastplate of righteousness, and having shod your feet with the preparation of the gospel of peace, above all, taking the shield of faith with which you will be able to quench all the fiery darts of the wicked one. And take the helmet of salvation, and the sword of the Spirit, which is the word of God; praying always with all prayer and supplication in the Spirit, being watchful to this end with all perseverance and supplication for all the saints—and for me, that utterance may be given to me, that I may open my mouth boldly to make known the mystery of the gospel, for which I am an ambassador in chains, that in it I may speak boldly, as I ought to speak (Ephesians 6:10–20).*

Paul closed his letter to the Ephesians with a three-fold call: put on Christ, stand strong against the devil, and pray.

The early church was acutely aware of the power of the devil—all manifestations and forms of wickedness—and the continual efforts of the enemy to destroy them. They knew that the devil dealt mainly in deceit and temptation. Paul reminded the Ephesians that they also knew the antidote for all deceit and temptation: the truth of Christ and the power of the Holy Spirit.

Pieces of armor—like those of the Roman soldiers—became Paul's metaphor for the nature and power of Christ Jesus. Our true armor is not physical armor against a physical enemy; neither is it manmade armor against human fleshly desires. It is spiritual armor, the *armor of God*, for spiritual protection and victory. Each piece refers specifically to one aspect of a believer's relationship with Christ:

GIRDLE OF TRUTH—the girdle was a piece of protective leather that covered the entire abdominal area, including the loins. This area of the body was believed by the Greeks to be the center of both a person's strength and creative power. The truth of Christ, revealed by the Spirit of Truth, gives us strength—the truth is to govern all that we creatively do and say, which includes every utterance we make.

BREASTPLATE OF RIGHTEOUSNESS—the breastplate covered the vital organs, heart and lungs. Both represented *life*—a heart beating according to God's direction and will, the lungs inhaling God's Spirit and exhaling the believer's witness. Righteousness is being in "right standing" with God, obeying His will and being reconciled to Him in love and forgiveness. Our righteousness was won by Christ Jesus on the cross, and in believing in Him, His righteousness covers our lives. We must set our hearts always toward doing what is right in God's eyes, and speak the words He gives us to speak.

FOOTWEAR OF THE PREPARATION OF THE GOSPEL OF PEACE—our feet connect us to the earth; this footwear speaks of the attitude we are to have as we walk about in a sinful world. We must prepare ourselves to walk as Jesus walked—to go where He leads with the anticipation that we will bring the Gospel to whomever we encounter. We must set our minds toward that goal each day: where is the Spirit leading me to go so I might share the Gospel of Jesus Christ with those I encounter? It is only in Christ that a person truly can know peace with God.

SHIELD OF FAITH—this is the faith we have in God, our protector. We have the ability to *choose* to believe God's truth and omnipotence (all-powerful nature), rather than believe in the devil's lies and threats. This shield was large, almost door-size. It covered the entire person and when wet, could quench fire arrows. Fiery darts were much feared in the ancient world. The devil's tactic against us is to strike paralyzing fear and doubt into our minds and hearts. It is by our faith that we withstand bouts of fear and doubt!

As soldiers stood side by side, their shields created almost an impenetrable "wall" that allowed the soldiers to move forward, and simultaneously forced the enemy to retreat. Faith in the church works the same way—it allows us to advance in winning the lost!

HELMET OF SALVATION—the helmet covered the brain, and thus, the mind and memory. We must never forget what Jesus did for us on the cross. We must never forget that our salvation brings with it the renewal of our minds by the power of the Holy Spirit. We must seek to think the thoughts of Christ and make decisions and choices daily that enact what Jesus desires to be said and done on this earth.

SWORD OF THE SPIRIT, THE WORD OF GOD—the sword is the only offensive weapon Paul mentioned. In battle, the swords of the soldiers were thrust through the very narrow space that existed between the shields of soldiers standing shoulder to shoulder. The advancing wall of shielded soldiers, with swords positioned every three to four feet, was an awesome threat to the enemy. The Word of God, when spoken under the inspiration of God's spirit, replaces lie with truth, insult with blessing, and threat with an invitation to God's forgiveness. The Word is powerful. It cuts to the core of life. We are to speak it aloud at every opportunity, and in concert with fellow believers. It is as we speak God's Word in unison as the body of Christ that we truly impact our society with truth.

Fully clothed in such armor, the Ephesians were commanded to stand firm. They were to remain solid in their convictions and in their united relationship. They were not to break rank. And as they moved forward against the enemy of their souls, they were not to remain silent. Paul admonished them to *pray*. Petition God! Request God's protection for all the saints. Seek and receive God's direction. Ask for God's courage and boldness in speaking the Gospel.

What an amazing picture Paul creates in just a few words!

This is the way we survive spiritually in a world tainted with sin and ruled by the devil's lies.

Are you aware today that the enemy of your souls is real and that you are always facing a very real assault from him?

Are you reminding yourself daily of all that you have received from Christ, and all that you *are* in Christ Jesus?

Are you praying continually for God's help?

A
Application for Today

There is an old saying, "All dressed up with no place to go."

How many times does this statement ring true for us—sadly so—whether individually or collectively as the church?

We have put our best face forward—with the finest in clothing, makeup, and hairstyle. We prepare our lives with the finest education and seek to develop our skills to climb as high as we can climb on the corporate or social ladder of our choice. But we attend no event worthy of the best we have to give.

Our choice of luxury car sits in the driveway of our dream home. But we rarely use our car or home to help others.

The church we attend is beautifully adorned inside and out. But no real "eternal transactions" are taking place.

As has been said in some circles, "We are all show and no go."

Paul did not teach the Ephesians to "dress up" in Christ solely for their sake, but for the eternal purposes of God throughout the world.

Our putting on Christ's nature is one strong aspect of our witness that God desires to use as a means to forgive and restore all mankind to Himself. People should be able to look at our lives—our behavior, our speech, our character displayed—and to see how we handle our material resources, and see in us a reflection of Christ's own nature and priorities.

Our advancing in Christ's power is the second strong aspect of our witness that God desires to defeat the enemy so that His kingdom might advance on this earth. We are to be people who are taking forward-motion risks with our faith, united strongly with other believers of like mind and purpose. We are to speak God's Word at every opportunity to win the lost and edify the saints.

Do you know your purpose today on this earth? Are you aligned with other believers of like purpose?

Do you know why you are here and what you are to do—not only in cosmic, long-range terms but *today*?

Above all, God desires that you become more and more like Christ Jesus, allowing Him to work in you to touch a lost world.

S
Supplementary Scriptures to Consider

Paul wrote similar words of admonition to the Thessalonians:

> You are all sons of light and sons of the day. We are not of the night nor of darkness. Therefore let us not sleep, as others do, but let us watch and be sober. For those who sleep, sleep at night, and those who get drunk are drunk at night. But let us who are of the day be sober, putting on the breastplate of faith and love, and as a helmet the hope of salvation. For God did not appoint us to wrath, but to obtain salvation through our Lord Jesus Christ (1 Thessalonians 5:5–9).

• What does it mean to you to be a "*son* of light"? What does it mean to be a "*son* of the day"? Keep in mind that light refers to inner spiritual light. Day is the time when work and transactions are accomplished, and when a person's life can be viewed most clearly by others.

- How do faith, love, and the hope of salvation attract others, rather than produce anger or resentment in them?

Paul also wrote this about vigilant prayer:

> Continue earnestly in prayer, being vigilant in it with thanks-giving; meanwhile praying also for us, that God would open to us a door for the word, to speak the mystery of Christ, for which I am also in chains, that I may make it manifest, as I ought to speak (Colossians 4:2–4).

- What does it mean to you to "continue earnestly" in prayer?

- What challenges do you face personally in being "vigilant" in prayer?

• What does it mean to be earnest and vigilant in prayer "with thanksgiving"? How does thanksgiving change the tenor of our petitions to God?

• Paul requested prayer for boldness in sharing the gospel, even as he sat in prison, bound by chains. He did not request freedom, but courage and the ability to speak clearly to his captors and fellow prisoners. How might this relate to your life?

I

Introspection and Implications

1. Can we ever escape the "wiles" of the devil against us?

2. How vulnerable is a person who does not put on the whole armor of God continually? How vulnerable is a person who dons the whole armor of God, but seeks to fight any spiritual battle alone?

3. In what ways have you struggled to maintain a vigilant and effective prayer life? How do you maintain consistency in prayer?

4. When we find ourselves being assaulted by fear or doubt, what should our recourse be? How might we help others who are struggling with fear or doubt?

C
Communicating the Good News

How important is it that we seek to win the lost *as a church*? In what ways might our evangelistic efforts be more effective if we allowed the Holy Spirit to unite all of the talents and abilities resident in the church?

What happens when a church fails to pray for its leaders to remain bold in their preaching and teaching of the Gospel?

What is the role of prayer in evangelism?

NOTES TO LEADERS
OF SMALL GROUPS

As the leader of a small discussion group, think of yourself as a facilitator with three main roles:

- Get the discussion started

- Involve every person in the group

- Encourage an open, candid discussion that remains Bible focused

You certainly don't need to be the person with all the answers! In truth, much of your role is to be a person who asks questions:

- What really impacted you most in this lesson?

- Was there a particular part of the lesson, or a question, that you found troubling?

- Was there a particular part of the lesson that you found encouraging or insightful?

- Was there a particular part of the lesson that you'd like to explore further?

Express to the group at the outset of your study that your goal as group is to gain new insights into God's Word—this is not the forum for defending a point of doctrine or a theological opinion. Stay focused on what God's Word says and means. The purpose of the study is also to share insights on how to apply God's Word to everyday life. *Every* person in the group can and should contribute—the collective wisdom that flows from Bible-focused discussion is often very rich and deep.

Seek to create an environment in which every member of the group feels free to ask questions of other members in order to gain greater understanding. Encourage the group members to voice their appreciation to one another for new insights gained, and to be supportive of one another personally. Take the lead in doing this. Genuinely appreciate and value the contributions made by each person.

You may want to begin each study by having one or more members of the group read through the section provided under "Bible Focus." Ask the group specifically if it desires to discuss any of the questions under the "Application" section...the "Supplemental Scriptures" section...and the "Implications" and "Communicating the Gospel" section. You do not need to bring closure—or come to a definitive conclusion or consensus—about any one question asked in this study. Rather, encourage your group that if the group does not *have* a satisfactory Bible-based answer to a question that the group engage in further "asking...seeking...and knocking" strategies to discover the answers! Remember the words of Jesus: "Ask, and it will be given to you, seek, and you will find; knock, and it will be opened to you. For everyone who asks receives, and he who seeks finds, and to him who knocks it will be opened" (Matthew 7:7–8).

Finally, open and close your study with prayer. Ask the Holy Spirit, whom Jesus called the Spirit of Truth, to guide your discussion and to reveal what is of eternal benefit to you individually and as a group. As you close your study, ask the Holy Spirit to seal to your remembrance what you have read and studied, and to show you ways in the upcoming days, weeks, and months *how* to apply what you have studied to your daily life and relationships.

General Themes for the Lessons

Each lesson in this study has one or more core themes. Continually pull the group back to these themes. You can do this by asking simple questions, such as, "How does that relate to _____?" . . . "How does that help us better understand the concept of _____?" . . . "In what ways does that help us apply the principle of _____?"

A summary of general themes or concepts in each lesson is provided below:

Lesson #1
GIFTED WITH SPIRITUAL WISDOM
Natural wisdom vs. spiritual wisdom
The hope of our calling in Christ
The value God holds for each of us as believers
The greatness of God's power extended to us

Lesson #2:
SAVED BY FAITH, NOT WORKS
Salvation
God's grace
Faith vs. works

Lesson #3:
UNITED IN CHRIST
Overcoming prejudices
Resolving differences
Seeking unity in Christ

Lesson #4:
EQUIPPED FOR MINISTRY
The role of the clergy
The role of the laity
Equipped for ministry
Edification

Lesson #5:
WALKING IN NEWNESS OF LIFE
Discerning right from wrong
Knowing what is acceptable to the Lord
Identifying "unfruitful works of darkness"
Avoiding evil

Lesson #6:
SUBMITTED TO ONE ANOTHER
Being filled continually with the spirit
The role of joy in the church
Praise and thanksgiving
Submission to God
Submission to other believers
Submission in family relationships

Lesson #7:
FULLY ARMED FOR SPIRITUAL BATTLE
The wiles and methods of the devil
Spiritual battles
The armor of God
Vigilance in prayer

NOTES

NOTES

NOTES

NOTES

NOTES

NOTES

NOTES

CPSIA information can be obtained
at www.ICGtesting.com
Printed in the USA
LVHW042112060221
678616LV00036B/1001